Conversations on/for South Asia

Intersections in Sociology, Art and Art History

A Conversation with Parul Dave-Mukherji

Conversations on/for South Asia Series Editors:

Sasanka Perera

Ravi Kumar

Dev Pathak

Bio-note on the editor:

Dev Nath Pathak teaches Sociology at South Asian University in New Delhi. He obtained doctorate in sociology at Jawaharlal Nehru University for his research on Maithili folksongs. His current research interests include themes in performative South Asia, education and studies in emotional meanings. He has contributed articles to various journals and chapters in edited books. He is currently the Reviews Editor of *Society and Culture in South Asia* (the journal of Department of Sociology, South Asian University, copublished with Sage India). He was Charles Wallace Fellow-2015 at Queen's University, Belfast. He can be reached at *dev@soc.sau.ac.in*.

Titles in the Series

Debating the Ancient and Present: A Conversation with Romila Thapar, edited by Sasanka Perera, 2015

The Question of South Asia -- Reflections, Rhetoric and the Idea of a University: A Conversation with Imtiaz Ahmad, edited by Ravi Kumar (Forthcoming)

Politics, Religion and Nation: A Convesation with Vasudha Dalmia, edited by Dev Nath Pathak (Forthcoming)

Conversations on/for South Asia

Intersections in Sociology, Art and Art History

A Conversation with Parul Dave-Mukherji

Edited by
Dev Nath Pathak

SAU
SOUTH ASIAN UNIVERSITY
Sociology@SAU

AAKAR

INTERSECTIONS IN SOCIOLOGY, ART AND ART HISTORY
A Conversation with Parul Dave-Mukherji
Edited by Dev Nath Pathak

First Published 2016

ISBN 978-93-5002-441-6

Published by
AAKAR BOOKS
28 E Pocket IV, Mayur Vihar Phase I, Delhi 110 091
Phones: 011 2279 5505, 2279 5641
Email: aakarbooks@gmail.com

In association with
Department of Sociology
Faculty of Social Sciences
South Asian University
Akbar Bhavan, Chanakyapuri,
New Delhi 110 021, India
Email: sociology@soc.sau.ac.in

Printed at
Saurabh Printers Pvt. Ltd.

Contents

Series Note

Conversations on/for South Asia

The Department of Sociology at South Asian University was established in 2011 within the Faculty of Social Sciences. In defining its vision and approach to teaching and research, the Department of Sociology notes on its website that it is "acutely aware of the non-existence of regular and serious forums for South Asian scholarship in social sciences to showcase our own research and thinking." This series is an effort on the part of the Department to create a platform of critical knowledge on issues that have been vital to South Asia.

As a series, *Conversations on/for South Asia* intends to keep itself open-ended, more so keeping in mind the necessity of inventing and re-inventing scholarship in and around ever dynamic South Asian societies. The series would not only publish conversations with South Asian scholars on vital issues of concern but would also be open to publishing other kinds of texts that contribute to a critical understanding of the region whose definition, intellectually, is mired in numerous debates and anxieties. It is one of the textual tools through which the Department of Sociology hopes to expand its thinking to the wider public domain in South Asia and the world in addition to its journal, *Society and Culture in South Asia*.

Each instalment in the series will be published under the editorial responsibility of one of the series' editors.

Preface and Acknowledgements

Intersections of Sociology, Art and Art History: A Conversation with Parul Dave-Mukherji is the second instalment, following *Debating the Ancient and Present: A Conversation with Romila Thapar*, in the publication series, 'Conversations on/for South Asia' launched by the Department of Sociology at South Asian University in 2015. This is based on the conversation which was organized by the Department of Sociology on 29 August 2014 at the Akbar Bhawan campus of South Asian University. The process that entailed preparation towards this conversation was the same as the first conversation in this series. It meant inviting interested scholars to submit questions in advance, arranging them thematically, and executing the conversation. The questions were formulated in the light of some of the publications of Prof. Parul Dave-Mukherji although not in a restricted sense. The details of these publications can be accessed at http://www.jnu.ac.in/Faculty/pdmukherji/.

Being a recently established Department of Sociology at the newly founded South Asian University, we have grappled with questions about the nature and scope of our discipline and its subject-matter extensively. In the ongoing pursuit as a collective of sociologists and social anthropologists, we tend to ask: what sociology and social anthropology means to us given the qualitative distinction of our institutional location? Coupled with the institutional location, we are also aware of the qualitative distinction of our intellectual orientation. It indeed aids in approaching the question of disciplinary boundaries with optimum reflexivity. We thus encounter somewhat self-evident intersections between sociology and social anthropology with various other fields of enquiries. This conversation reflects our ongoing pursuits.

My colleagues in the Department of Sociology ought to be acknowledged for keeping such a pursuit alive and promising. I also need to thank them for making a conscious effort to steward the paradigm of intellectual and academic progress intricately linked with the institutional progress of the Department of Sociology. Various propositions emerging from the meetings of the Department have explicitly stressed the relation of the individual and institution in most of our academic and extra-academic activities. The Conversation Programme of the Department is one of the manifest examples among various others. Departmental endeavours of this kind, while adding to the intellectual progress of individual members, also reflect upon the whole Departmental collective. This is crucial at a time characterized by the reduction of academic pursuits into atomized phenomena.

Intersections of sociology with arts and art history is one of the central issues for some of us. Prof. Sasanka Perera has been instrumental in highlighting the imperative to construe these intersections not only with art but also with other potentially sidelined fields. This was the reason why he was an ideal option to chair and moderate this conversation. I thank him for undertaking it with utmost enthusiasm. I would also extend my gratitude to my colleagues for engendering a consensus about the pursuit of such intersections, a tangible anchor in the midst of the fogginess of interdisciplinarity and its many cognates.

This conversation with Parul Dave-Mukherji, located in the above scheme, is a humble beginning and contribution to the explorations of disciplinary intersections. This is the first formal event along the lines of intersections on art, sociology and art history , among many of our informal endeavours. I must acknowledge the deep interest of Parul Dave-Mukherji in the idea of this conversation, its execution, and finally in the publication of the conversation. She affirmed our faith that disciplinary boundaries are not too tight to prevent dialogues.

Like in many of our earlier events, this too witnessed our students' active interest and dynamic roles. Our former student, Kanika Rai Dhanda ensured that some of the crucial publications of Parul Dave-Mukherji are available for consultation by students and colleagues who wanted to participate in the conversation with their questions. She deftly coordinated the marathon preparation for the event as well as the conversation itself on the day of the event. Apoorva Kaul and Ratan Kumar Roy were equally significant in scripting the event. They ensured that the experience of this conversation, on the intersections of sociology and arts, is not devoid of artistic feelings. It included Ratan Kumar Roy's posters of the events and curated sound tracks during the conversation. Like most of our events in the Department of Sociology, this too vindicated my long cherished idea: academic events must be curated with students' perspectives, energy, and imagination, and if not, they would merely become boring rituals. I must warmly thank our students for paving the way for disciplinary enchantments with their dynamic interventions in our programmes. In the same vein, I acknowledge the role of the staff in the Faculty of Social Sciences, namely Samson George, Aman Kumar, and Jyoti Chawla. The credit for successful logistical arrangements behind our events goes entirely to FSS support staffers.

In formulating the text for publishing, we have edited it minimally, keeping the spirit, the feel and the nuances of the conversation intact. The manuscript has gone through a grinding editorial reading, peer-reviews, and reworking. I thank Parul Dave-Mukherji for taking time off from her hectic schedule and reading and correcting the manuscript. I also wish to acknowledge the significant role of Sasanka Perera in shaping the introductory outline. A critical reading of the manuscript by Ravi Kumar enhanced in the accessibility of the text. And, I would add Ektaa Jain, a research scholar in sociology at the Centre for the Study of Social Systems, Jawaharlal Nehru University, for the careful proof-reading of the manuscript. I acknowledge the contributions by the participants who added significance to the conversation with their distinct questions, namely: Apoorva Kaul, Dev Pathak, Kanika Rai Dhanda, Manoj Kumar Dhakal, Parul Dave-Mukherji, Pooja Kalita, Ratan Kumar Roy and Sasanka Perera.

Last but not the least, I sincerely acknowledge the creative efforts of Anoli Perera, a noted contemporary visual artist from Sri Lanka, in designing the cover for the present instalment as well as for the series.

New Delhi
30 November 2015

Dev Pathak
Department of Sociology
Faculty of Social Sciences
South Asian University

Introduction:
A Brief Outline of the Context of the Conversation[1]

The contextual relevance of this conversation alludes to broadly two domains of reasoning. One is a practical domain, located in the Department of Sociology at South Asian University (SAU). And the other is a conceptual-discursive domain emanating from the perusal of a selection of literature pertaining to the issue of the relation between sociology and art as well as the conversation between sociologists and art historians. This outline will present an eagle's view of the conceptual-discursive domain in the latter part. But, the practical domain, close to the teachers and students of sociology at SAU is not devoid of conceptual, practical and disciplinary visions. The Department of Sociology cherishes the ideal of sociology in conversation with myriad other disciplines from the region, in a framework which is optimally inclusive of various traditions and modes of reasoning. As the vision-statement of the Department reads:

> The Department creates a forum for the *newer forms of knowledge* that comprehends and represents the South Asian context with

1. The conversation was organized by Rickshaw: A Students' Collective, Department of Sociology, South Asian University, on 29 August 2014, and moderated by Sasanka Perera, Professor in Sociology at South Asian University. The conversation was conceived and coordinated by Dev Pathak.

> a more authoritative and nuanced voice. We strongly believe in the need to actively intervene in the process of knowledge formation through a *constant sharing of knowledge that the region produces as well as through interaction with the world beyond the region*[2] (emphasis added).

The sections emphasized in italics adequately hint at the practical relevance of this conversation. It enables us to fathom the necessity of keeping the disciplinary boundaries flexible enough for sustained interactions with various other disciplines. In our pursuit of *newer forms of knowledge*, therefore, we ought to be flexible not only with regard to geo-political but also in respect of disciplinary boundaries. The practical necessity of such an interactive arrival at *newer forms of knowledge* also arises from a valid aspiration for the humanistic nature in sociological enquiries. Young researchers from across the region sometimes aspire to research into various cultural issues, connecting them with the world of arts. This summons the need to think beyond the familiar and well-trodden areas of conventional sociological enquiry. The issue is well articulated at the outset of the contextualization of this conversation by Sasanka Perera, who moderated this conversation. Such practical imperatives, amongst others, are also crucial in maintaining the humanistic contours of sociology at the Department. This was also instrumental in another conversation titled *Art, Artists and Social Sciences*[3] that the Department organized recently. In short, this is about stimulating ourselves in the

2. See http://www.sau.int/sociology.html (last visited on 10 November 2015).
3. The Department of Sociology, SAU conducted this conversation on 20 August 2015 with Prof. Venka Purushothaman and Prof. Roma Chatterji. See https://www.facebook.com/events/395836463953703/ (last visited on 10 November 2015)

practice of sociology to engage with the objects of arts and their contexts of production and consumption without falling prey to 'disciplinary gate-keeping' on the thematic of research based on reductionist notions of disciplinary borders. Moreover, conversations of this kind also make pedagogic sense in the scheme of designing our courses, devising our pedagogy in general, and creating novel avenues in our teaching and learning programmes. This is a modest way of bridging the disciplinary gaps which have distanced, allegedly, social sciences from the domain of art, artists and the intricate issues linked to these. In addition to this practical context of the relevance of this conversation, there is a fairly daunting discursive terrain which solicits attention, at least a cursory sketch as the following.

The idea of a conversation between art historians and sociologists stem from a discursive realization, which is broadly two-fold. One is primarily due to the shared disciplinary and aesthetic interests in artworks. In an ideal sense, the mutuality of interest is an abiding feature of the contemporary discourses in sociology and art history, and it has an explicit but a not so popular disciplinary lineage. And the other pertains to the epistemological divides, a fallout of the fortification of science against arts. Most self-reflective discussions offer a critical point of departure from this divide.

This two-fold realization is as old as the days when social scientists imagined the arrival of a proverbial Newton to render social science disciplines more 'scientific' than, perhaps, they could be. The emergence and subsequent bolstering of scientific epistemology rendered 'scientific as the only legitimate form of knowing'. Many philosophers and historians of science debated against the phenomenon of scientism eclipsing multiple other, equally legitimate, ways of knowing. Since it is debatable whether these discussions have made any difference in the prevailing fundamental attitudes, there is an imperative to repeat the question of the relation between art and social sciences, time and again. This question holds additional significance at a time when the sub-discipline, 'sociology of art' is turning a new leaf and aspiring to become 'new sociology of art' with novel promises and departures from erstwhile preoccupations.[4] But even so, this does not mean that the sociology of art has acquired the kind of intellectual popularity, legitimacy and institutionalization which older sub-disciplines such as sociology of medicine and urban sociology have.

More importantly, the question could be deemed of discursive value in contemporary sociological scholarship in the region—how is art of interest to sociology? And perhaps the seeming 'innocence' of this question could reveal the state of sociology, if not in universal at least in the particular regional sense. The state of sociology in South Asia that de-recognizes artworks and their contexts of production and consumption, or puts them in disciplinary margins as a 'soft' and unquantifiable field of enquiry, is unfortunately oblivious of the history of the discipline in the region. The sociological problem with art also hinges on an epistemological problem, a contestation over the role of 'experience' in the domain of science. There have been sincere attempts to contest the problem, at macro as well as micro levels of the disciplinary history. This contestation, and its epistemological implications at the global level, began to appear ever since the advent of the 'positivistic dispute'[5]. The

4. This important aspect is given a detailed deliberation in the latter part of the introduction. The mainstay of the idea behind the new sociology of art comes from Eduardo de la Fuente's (2007) detailed perusal of the developments in sociology and art history.
5. In the context of this dispute, particularly in the context of German sociology, an effort was made to formulate an agenda

latter aimed at puncturing 'hypostatized configuration of science' and thereby overcoming the delimiting impact of scientism. In short, it opened up the possibility of including 'experience' as an important category in pursuits of knowledge. This assumed a more radical articulation with the advocacy of 'methodological pluralism'[6] qua anarchy as essential characteristics of the ways of knowing.

Experience, the most basic category in the debates on science and arts, was the muse for philosophers ever since the so-called beginning of scientific epistemology[7]. However, a systematic critical stock of the separation of art and science, experience and aesthetics, emerges with John Dewey's emphasis on the significance of 'art as experience'[8], and it's indispensable location in the scientific (read, rational and progressive) framework.

Way back in 1934, Dewey critically noted, "art is remitted to a separate realm, where it is cut off from the association with the materials and aims of every other form of human effort, undergoing, and achievement...Mountain peaks do not float unsupported; they do not even just rest upon the earth. They are the earth in one of its manifest operations" (1934: 3).

Dewey helped us fathom the problems of the so-called 'expert knowledge on art' by suggesting that any theory or philosophy of art is sterilized unless it makes us aware of

---

for puncturing the 'hypostatized configuration of science', and to overcome the delimiting impact of scientism. See Adorno et al. (1981).

6. See Feyerabend (2010).
7. Bertrand Russell eloquently places a radically subjective notion of experience in the inception of scientific epistemology starting with Rene Descartes's meditations. See Russell (2013).
8. See Dewey (1934).

the function of art in relation to other modes of experience. In this scheme, 'aesthetic experience' is not an esoteric realization; instead, it belongs to everyday life of ordinary folks as well as artists. To deliver a blow to the arrogance of art-experts, Dewey argues, "it is mere ignorance that leads then to the supposition that connection of art and aesthetic perception with experience signifies a lowering of their significance and dignity" (Ibid.: 19).

By implication, Dewey underlined the necessity of engaging with artworks, artifacts of cultural experiences in general, without allowing disciplinary arrogance to retard the production of knowledge. The very nature of aesthetic experience solicits an interdisciplinary approach, an inevitable need in understanding art and aesthetics. This is the insight, which enables a sociologist to ask critically as to why "prior to the 1970s, most sociologists who dealt with the arts were 'viewed as intellectuals in the broad sense or as radicals, but not really proper sociologists'" (De la Fuente 2007: 410).

However, from among those few radical sociologists, there emanated a nuanced approach towards comprehending the category of art. In this regard, it is relevant to recall the propositions of Nisbet made at a time which was characterized by a 'crisis in Western sociology'[9]. Bolstering a case for 'Sociology as an Art Form', Nisbet suggests,

> How alike are the sociologist's and artist's efforts to endow subject matter with what Herbert Read, the art historian and critic, has called "the illusion of motion". No mean esthetic

---

9. In his thought-provoking work, Gouldner underlined a crisis in the prevalent ways of doing (teaching, researching and writing) sociology, and advocated an imperative for a 'new' and more reflexive sociology, which could steer clear of the dominant ways. See Gouldner (1970).

> skill is involved in Marx's depiction of capitalism as a structure in motion, in Tocqueville's rendering of equality as a dynamic process, or Weber's of rationalization... We cannot take away from Tocqueville, Marx, Weber and the other sociologists the visions for which they are famous...but we live in ignorance if we do not see clearly these same visions, albeit stated differently, in the earlier writings of such minds as Burke, Blake, Carlyle, Balzac...(1976:7-8).

There is an essential unity of art and science, no matter how eclipsed it may seem in the wake of politics which separate the two. Presenting a prophylaxis against scientism, rather than science, to emphasize the unity of science and art, Nisbet suggests, "when Kepler wrote, "the roads by which men arrive at their insights into celestial matters seem to me almost as worthy of wonder as those matters themselves", it would never have occurred to him that there was any significant difference between what he, the theologian, the philosopher, and the artist were engaged in" (ibid.: 4-5).

In his work, Nisbet enlists a a number of common thematic ideas in social sciences in the 19th century, such as community, masses, power, development, progress, conflict, egalitarianism, anomie, alienation and disorganization. He also suggests that there are identical themes in the world of art—painting, literature, even music. Social scientists have benefited from their engagement with works of art and in comprehending thematic realities. To make it more explicit, Nisbet surmises,

> Scientists Marx, Weber, Durkheim, and Simmel were without question. But they were also artists, and had they not been artists, had they contented themselves with demonstrating solely what had been arrived at through aseptic problem design, through meticulous verification, and through constructions of theory which pass muster in a graduate course in methodology of sociology today, the entire world of thought would be much poorer (ibid.: 7).

Turning geopolitically inward, the sociological inclination towards art was not absent in the sociology in South Asia though its influence has been historically muted. To be more microscopic, and look at the Indian context for mere heuristic convenience, there were a number of sociologists in India reasoning with the relation of art and society in the early phase of disciplinary development. It is relevant to briefly allude to the extensive deliberations of Radhakamal Mukerjee[10], one of the pioneering thinkers setting the temperament of sociology in India. It is curious to note that Mukerjee, mostly noted for presenting a sociological challenge to the predominance of positivism of economics, wrote a number of well-known essays on the issue of art and its relation with society, civilization, religion, and polity. One of the essays titled "The Meaning and Evolution of Art in Society"[11], published in the *American Sociological Review*, was accompanied by an added note from the editor of the journal:

> The Editors think that American sociologists will be interested in the contemporary thinking of an eminent Indian sociologist in the eventful year of 1945 (1945: 496).

It was evident that the world at large was curious about an Indian sociologist's venture into the domain of art. And that attention perhaps came with the realization that Western sociology hardly paid serious attention to art at this time. Indeed, it was only a couple of decades later that the 'crisis in Western sociology' referred to above became pronounced. However, before it was pronounced, Mukerjee in India had articulated,

> Art is at once a social product and an established means of social control… Modern sociologists should now vindicate the

10. There have been a few noticeable attempts to systematically understand the contribution of Mukerjee to sociology in the Indian context. See for example, Thakur (2015).
11. See Mukerjee (1945).

> importance of this fertile field—the study of art forms as the unchecked efflorescence and clarified utterance of culture, as its principal measure, directive force as well as means of control (Ibid.: 496-497).

Let us now take a heuristic jump, and ask—'then what happened?' Could sociology in India persist with its engagement with the arts? Rather than attempting to answer such difficult questions, it is easier to quickly mention a curious development on the contemporary discursive trope in India. Many years after Gouldner's announcement of crisis in Western sociology, some sociologists in India began to pronounce their own 'crises'[12]. This notion of crises was mostly characterized by the motif of 'lament' on the allegedly deplorable condition of teaching, research and writing in sociology in India. This was more succinctly underlined in Vasavi's proposition that sociology in India is "fragmented and diluted, unable to forge an identity of its own, respond to changing times, and generate new schools of theory, methods and perspectives" (2011: 402). Did this announcement of crises in sociology in India lead to any call for a 'new sociology', like that of Gouldner? Or, does it augur to any other optimistic consequence of the realization of the crises? Perhaps the answer lies in the course of time that is yet to come rather in the times that have so far lapsed. But then, there is a curious observation to share, which unfortunately speaks of an ongoing separation of art and sociology in India. Take for example, some attempts by sociologists to recount the stories of pioneer sociologists. Madan has called it, while reproducing selected works of Radhakamal Mukerjee, an attempt to rescue pioneers from 'disciplinary amnesia.'[13] Curiously enough however, it hardly

12. See for example, Das (1993) and Deshpande (1994).
13. See Madan (2003).

takes note of Mukerjee's sustained engagement with the artifacts of cultural articulations. Does it mean there has been a strategy to keep the engagements with the arts and other civilizational entities by some pioneers away from the sociological framework when recounting the contributions of these pioneers?? This requires further investigation on some other occasion.

This is the broader scheme, presented briefly in the foregone, that makes a candid conversation on sociology, art, etc. a relevant exercise. Indeed, this is a modest beginning which solicits due perpetuity of bold ruminations and unhindered conversations amongst scholars from at least two disciplines, sociology and art history (the more the merrier).

This beginning is also pertinent at this juncture as art as well as history is stretching out for a novel realizations: the interaction of art with society! Papastergiadis' (2010) emphasis on artists' social interactions and complex patterns of cultural exchange in the backdrop of producing their artworks are expressive of this new realization amongst artists and art-historians. Artists too are in the fold of everyday life, and hence they are not in a social vacuum. This realization too is located in a discursive trope. A systematic recent thesis on the interaction of the social and the aesthetic, and therefore imperative of dialogue between sociologists, artists and art-historians, appeared with the publication of Becker's *Art Worlds.*[14] Becker tilled the ground for mutual disciplinary interest by critically departing from the conventional-dominant approaches in art history and art

14. Many name Howard Becker's *Art Worlds* and Pierre Bourdieu's *Distinction,* both published in the decade of the 1980s (1982 and 1984 respectively), as two significant works underlining the common ground for art history, sociology and cultural studies.

philosophy, arguing, "the dominant tradition takes the artists and art work, rather than the network of cooperation, as central to the analysis of art as a social phenomenon"[15]. Subsequently, sociologists interested in art also began to self-critically recognize the limitations of sociologists' interest in 'unmasking' artworks. All the indicators of connections between art and society, such as class, gender, dominant ideology, capital interest, market, etc., were handy tools in tearing apart what an art historian could have dubbed as the stylized presentation of aesthetics. This was typically expressed when Bourdieu suggested, "sociology and art do not make good bedfellows"[16]. However, there have been significant endeavours ever since to unravel a debate leading to an interesting realization. This has been summed up as a compelling message for both sociologists and art historians: an object of art is both, social and aesthetic, at once. This emphatically underscores the indispensability of conversations between art historians and sociologists, appearing in a tangible form in a volume titled *Art from Start to Finish* edited by Howard Becker, Piere-Michel Menger and Robert Faulkner (2006). This supports what de la Fuente has dubbed as the 'New Sociology of Art', 'confident enough to begin dialogue with other disciplines, such as art history and cultural studies, if and when these discourses share the assumption that art is a social construct, and its production and consumption are thoroughly social in character" (2007: 423). This proposition is resonant with Jeremy Tanner's (2003) endeavour to forge a relationship between sociologists and other scholars interested in art. And, importantly enough,

---

15. Becker quoted in Eduardo de la Fuente's The 'New Sociology of Art' (2007: 411).
16. Bourdieu quoted in Eduardo de la Fuente's The 'New Sociology of Art' (2007: 41).

this relationship, a kind of intellectual kinship, does not emerge in a theoretical vacuum. Tanner revisits, from the classical to the contemporary, theoretical framework in sociology, re-reading Durkheim, Marx, Weber, Simmel, Mannheim, Parsons, Elias and Habermas. This enables Tanner to propose that the best art history is, implicitly at least, sociologically informed, and the best sociology of art places questions of artistic agency and aesthetic form at the core of its research.

This is the brief outline of the discursive context, moot issues of shared concerns, which underlines the significance of the conversation between sociologists, art-historians and scholars of cultural studies, to name only three. The following conversation could perhaps amply show some of the issues flagged in this outline. It may reveal that scholars in sociology and social anthropology are keen to unravel the phenomenon of art-making without being restricted to issues of style and material. This particular tribe of gazers upon art tends to probe further into the constitution of meanings, going beyond the surface-value of style and materials. Seemingly, the materials in artworks is an anchor to the socio-cultural and hermeneutic politics for sociologists. And hence they keep asking for further meanings and as to how their ethnography on art and artists' activities varies from that of an art historian. Or maybe, the latter too adopts a similar attitude! And the disciplinary tribes thereby would hopefully arrive at a fertile ground that might enable them to respond to a conducive intellectual polyphony, apt in the time of pluralism of truth. The more we converse, the better we understand as to how sociologists and art historians are co-travellers on the same path.

REFERENCES

Adorno, T.W. et al. 1981. *The Positivist Dispute in German Sociology*. London: Ashgate.

Becker, H.S. 1982. *Art Worlds*. Berkeley and Los Angeles: University of California Press.

Becker, H.S., R.R. Faulkner, and B. Kirshenblatt-Gimblett, eds. 2006. *Art from Start to Finish: Jazz, Painting, and Other Improvisations*. Chicago and London: University of Chicago Press.

De la Fuente, E. 2007. The 'New Sociology of Art': Putting Art Back into Social Science Approaches to the Arts, *Cultural Sociology*, 1(3): 409-425.

Das, V. 1993. 'Sociological Research in India—The State of Crisis', *Economic and Political Weekly*, Vol. 28 (23): 1159-1161.

Deshpande, S. 1994. 'Crisis in Sociology: A Tired Discipline', *Economic and Political Weekly*, Vol. 29 (10): 575-576.

Dewey, J. 1934. *Art as Experience*. New York: Minton, Balch & Company.

Feyerabend, P. 2010. *Against Method*. London: Verso.

Gouldner, A. 1970. *The Coming Crisis in Western Sociology*. New York: Basic Books.

Madan, T.N. Ed. 2003. *Sociology at the University of Lucknow: The First Half Century, 1921-1975*. New Delhi: Oxford University Press.

Mukerjee, R. 1945. 'The Meaning and Evolution of Art in Society', *American Sociological Review*, 10: 4 (496-503).

Papastergiadis, N. 2010. *Spatial Aesthetics: Art, Place and the Everyday*. Amsterdam: Institute of Network Cultures.

Nisbet, R. 1976. *Sociology as an Art Form*. London: Oxford University Press.

Russell, B. 2013. *History of Western Philosophy*. London: Routledge.

Tanner, J. Ed. 2003. *The Sociology of Art: A Reader*. London: Routledge.

Thakur, M. 2015. *The Quest for Indian Sociology: Radhakamal Mukerjee and Our Times*. Shimla: Indian Institute of Advanced Studies.

Vasavi, A.R. 2011. "Pluralising the Sociology of India", *Contributions to Indian Sociology*, 45 (3): 399-426.

The Conversation

Sasanka Perera: I would like to thank Parul Mukherji for accepting our invitation to take part in this ongoing series and also to 'Rickshaw, a Students' Collective' at the Department of Sociology, South Asian University, for coming up with the idea of this conversation. To put this conversation in a specific context, I will start with a few brief observations. It can be confusing for many in the conventional sociological pursuits as to why a Department of Sociology is organizing a conversation with an art historian. This is not what sociologists and social anthropologists usually do. There are a few reasons underlying our interest in this conversation.

We supervise students' dissertations in the Masters Programme in Sociology. Some of these students have interests in art, both performing as well as visual arts. So, we invariably engage with the questions and issues pertaining to the arts. However, in these situations we have to wonder if we are intellectually equipped to work on questions about arts, artists, and many related themes? Have we thought of these matters? How would we bridge the gap between disciplines such as sociology, social anthropology, and art history? This is one one of the considerations that prompted us to think of this conversation.

As sociologists and social anthropologists, some of us have a passion for art. It could be an individual passion evolved in the course of our intellectual and academic journeys. Some of us translate our personal passions into an intellectual enterprise as well. In my case, I have been attempting to teach a course called 'Visual Art and the Politics of Social Transformation'. When I was trying to design the course a long time ago at the University of Colombo and when I was reworking the syllabus at Hitosubashi University in Tokyo in 2010, and started collecting the readings, one of the things that struck my mind was that very few people of my kind, sociologists and anthropologists, had written anything on art. So much so, the readings I selected were authored by art historians, curators and sometimes artists. I wondered as to why this was the case?

Why are we averse to engage with arts in our research and in our writings? Is it because sociology is somehow obsessed with the written and spoken word? Interests in the visual within sociology seems to be confined to a periphery of sociological writing and often imprisoned within visual anthropology and visual sociology. Or is there some kind of inherent methodological problem in sociology that does not allow practitioners to intellectually deal with the visual? Why is it absent in the so-called mainstream sociology and social anthropology?

When I came to Delhi and spoke with other colleagues who shared similar concerns, I asked my friend Roma Chatterji, Professor of Sociology at the University of Delhi, whose book on folk arts[17] had just come out: is this merely my imagination or do we have a problem as far as the absence of art in sociology is concerned? She informed me that it was not my imagination; this is indeed a problem worthy of

17. Roma Chatterji's book is titled *Speaking with Pictures: Folk Art and the Narrative Tradition in India* (published by Routledge, Delhi, 2012).

critical reflection; scholars in social sciences do not seem to be interested in art.

Subsequently, we had Iftikhar Dadi[18], an art historian from Cornell University, to deliver a special lecture at the Department of Sociology, South Asian University, on "Art and the Visual Public Sphere in Pakistan."[19] It was a very interesting lecture. But it contained components that, I realized, we could not grasp entirely due to various reasons including the disciplinary distance between sociology and art history. To be more precise, there were issues which for us needed further explanation. For example, Dadi's detailed discussion on artist Naiza Khan's interest in travelling to the streets of Karachi to work on her paintings of the female nudes attracted the attention of the sociologists in the audience. Dadi also pointed out that the character of Saddam Hussein was not so popular or respected in Pakistan till very recently. And yet suddenly, his image was mass-produced in a widely circulating postcard with religious connotations. But Hussein was never a religious man. The intellectual stimulation of the talk notwithstanding, Dadi's lecture left us without answers on many counts. For example, we were not sure as to why an artist's engagement with Saddam Hussein's image happened at that point in time in the political history of Pakistan and why the unknown artists had opted to use the figure of a non-religious Arab tyrant for a religious cause in Pakistan which involved mass produced popular

18. For more on Iftikar Dadi, please vist: http://arthistory.cornell.edu/people/dadi.cfm (last accessed on 30 August 2015).
19. The Iftikhar Dadi lecture was part of the 'Exploring South Asia Lecture Series' of the Department of Sociology, Faculty of Social Sciences at South Asian University and was held on 26 August 2013 at South Asian University, Akbar Bhawan, Chanakyapuri, New Delhi.

'art'? We were also not sure as to why Naiza Khan[20] was going to the tacky streets of Karachi to do her work, leaving behind the safety and comfort zone offered by her studio. What were deeper socio-cultural undercurrents of her street-art? Many similar questions required us to look at the works of art and an artist's manoeuvrings in different interrogative frameworks and in the specific contexts of their production and consumption. It made us realize that when we look at art, we might be asking slightly different kinds of questions due to our disciplinary orientation, whereas people in art history might be asking a different set of questions. Or the emphases in our questions were quite different.

For us, this is the brief background from our own recent interactions with art and sociology which provided the relevance for this conversation. More specifically, the conversation hinges upon a host of questions that we would be posing to Parul Mukherji, and thereby many levels of dialogue will hopefully ensue. To take the privilege of being the moderator of this conversation, I begin with some of my own questions.

I want to start with two issues; one is related to what I said before: the absence of sociologists' interest in looking at art. Along this line I wonder whether an art historian is the only legitimate person to socially and politically situate art in the wider context of its production, consumption and engagement. Second, we get the sense that history itself has its own intriguing nervousness when dealing with the present. Is this nervousness inherent in art history too? In other words, is art history adequately equipped in intellectual terms to deal with the present as opposed to something like

20. For a quick familiarity with Khan's art, see http://artasiapacific.com/Shop/Goods/NaizaKhan (last accessed on 11 September 2015).

sociology? I wonder if this could also take us to discuss the contemporary peculiarities in the domain of art.

Parul Dave-Mukherji: First of all, I would like to thank you all for inviting me; thanks to students for their proactive role in making this possible. I am very pleased to have seen the questions in advance which gave me a sense of the kind of concerns that you all are interested in. They touch upon a wide range of theoretical issues. This is more pertinent for me, since I am on a sabbatical, and these kinds of questions lead me to a mid-career retrospection. I will start with Prof. Perera's set of questions.

Is art history the only domain where the question of politics and art can be discussed? At the outset, I would like to make certain distinctions, i.e. the distinction between the traditional discipline of Art History and Visual Studies; the latter is an offshoot of Art History following its conversation with social sciences — that includes sociology. Visual Studies is more aligned with "New Art History"— a term that we embraced around 2000 in Baroda to signal a disciplinary re-orientation. This shift from art history to visual studies grew out of a disciplinary crisis; much like the crisis referred to by Sasanka Perera within Sociology in India. It is the same orientation towards new Art History that manifests itself in the nomenclature adopted by the Visual Studies Department in the School of Arts and Aesthetics, JNU. Jyotindra Jain, the founder of this School and trained in Visual Anthropology played a key role in the adoption of this nomenclature. Visual Studies also signals an alliance with cultural studies and postcolonial studies, and thus foregrounds cultural politics and political economy, among other issues.

Now let's take up the question about disciplinary unease that Sasanka Perera raised. It is akin to that of historians when they are asked to look at their own times. Their tools are built to help them focus on the past. This issue came up within

Art History in Baroda when we wanted to collapse the distinction between Art History and Art Criticism which were offered as disciplinary options within Art History: the first was meant to devote its attention to the art of the past while the latter, to that of the contemporary. It is this separation that had a stultifying effect on the discussion of the political in art.

I consider this unease in art history as productive—as something that keeps criticality alive. Its disappearance is alarming in the way art writing on contemporary art flourishes or art description on traditional art exists unproblematically in the age of disturbing identity politics. In the case of the former, a close nexus between private art galleries and the art market that underlie the publication of artists' monographs is obvious. The decline of state art institutions and publications associated with them have given rise to a gap increasingly filled by private art galleries—a phenomenon that cannot be just decried because there is no art without patronage. The 'celebrity monograph' of artists, which are published by private galleries and private art institutions leaves little scope for a critical reflection on where the discipline is going, the state of art, its relationship with the art market, global capitalism, art's relevance to community life or the public sphere.

Sasanka Perera: So how could we promote that sense of unease or disturbance?

Parul Dave-Mukherji: This may sound utopian, but if we strengthen the arms of the state art institutions like the Lalit Kala Akademi and the National Gallery of Modern Art, it might play a positive role. These days, "disturbance" may not have positive connotations, given the fact that many of our art institutions are in fact ailing, and are on the verge of dissolution. Hence this term has to be applied to the level of ideology to make us self-reflexive about deep divides within the social space—between the elite, English-speaking block which has high cultural capital and the vernacular, 'rurban' side, which has high creativity but limited power of verbal expression. Given the dominance of the art market, today there are limited spaces where these critical reflections are possible. Earlier, such places included the academia and state art institutions. But now, with the proliferation of a right wing ideology, the latter faces the threat of compromising their autonomy.

Sasanka Perera: When we talk about these issues, various possibilities related to the study of art come to my mind. The institutional collaboration towards concerted regional efforts in art-making is one such possibility, which to some extent has already taken place. Perhaps, we can come to this issue later. Let's take the next question, probably a shorter one.

Dev Pathak: In some of your writings you have indicated the necessity of being interdisciplinary, particularly when you intend to conceptually and theoretically revisit to unsettle some of the settled ideas. In this regard, you have emphasized the imperative of bringing in cultural anthropology within the purview of conceptual discussions in art history. Primarily, if one has to problematize the settled notions within a disciplinary framework, it is inevitable to turn to other sources of knowledge. And intellectual history of social science presents umpteen testimonials for this perspective—intellectual promiscuity is a precondition for intellectual growth!

In our times, we have vested this notion in the phrase of interdisciplinary or any other synonym of it. While the objective seems to be well-meaning in the light of the intellectual history of knowledge, one feels inclined to be a bit of a devil's advocate. How do we really perform the new found sacred practice of interdisciplinary studies? And if we do perform it, by an eclectic juxtaposition of various strands from different disciplines, how do we retain the basic wherewithal arising from the parent discipline? Being a young academic, I have personally met with situations of stalemate in this regard. I debate with my friends and foes as to how we can be interdisciplinary without losing sight of the disciplinary fundamentals.

I must mention an instance for this. I hear from some of my colleagues, particularly of my age group, who teach at schools of arts and aesthetics—that too much social science is being smuggled into performance studies! And I get a sense that my personal anxiety and dilemma are actually very public, perhaps historical. How do we find that Archimedean point? A silly idea it may seem though, whereby we could be interdisciplinary without the discomfort of being so. In other words, we could blissfully indulge in promiscuity without any guilt of violating the rule of disciplinary monogamy.

It is also meaningful to ask you: What kind of dialogue or exchanges could you possibly imagine between disciplines, say for example, art history, visual studies, performance studies, anthropology of art and performance etc.?

Parul Dave-Mukherji: If you call this a short question, I don't know what to expect of the next [laughter]. It reminds me of Suzanne Langer's famous dictum: "There are no happy marriages in art—only successful rape."[21] Today, we are far ahead in this purist, and formalist understanding of genres and it is interdisciplinarity which is a given, and its enormous cognitive impact stands acknowledged, as noted by Clifford

21. Suzanne Langer, *Problems in Art* (New York: Scribner, 1957); pp. 86.

Geertz as early as the 1980s: "Something is happening to the way we think about the way we think!"[22]

However, in pedagogic practice, I am very cautious about interdisciplinarity and would like to qualify that there are good and bad ways of performing interdisciplinarity. I will start with the bad ways, that is, when interdisciplinarity is used to take a short cut between, say, two disciplines so that the difficulty of comprehending their mutual inflection is evaded. In this case, one does not lose one's bearings on encountering another discipline but simply flits from one discipline to the other at the cost of rigour. The good way of interdisciplinarity is when one grounds oneself in any one discipline and interrogates the other disciplines. For example, when I ventured into Performance Studies from Art History while critiquing an expert of Performance Studies, Richard Schechner's take on *rasa*[23], my issue was Schechner's implicit distinction between the West and the rest. This inadvertently led me to move towards anthropology. However, my questions about visual representation stemmed from within the disciplinary matrix of Visual Studies. 'Interdisciplinary' works better when one does not cross boundaries of disciplines with a preordained programme of crossing boundaries. Paradoxically, the more grounded one is in one's discipline, attending to its own historicity and disciplinary specificities, the more one feels the need to traverse elsewhere. As one's discipline expands

22. Clifford Geertz, 'Blurred Genres: the Refiguration of Social Thought in Local Knowledge', *Further Essays in Interpretative Anthropology* (New York, NY: Basic Books, 1983); pp. 20.
23. 'Bodies, Power and Difference: Representations of the East-West Divide in the Study of Indian Aesthetics', *The Body/Le Corps/Der Korper/Telo, Filosofski Vestnik* XXIII, 2/2002, Ljubljana, Slovenia, pp. 205-220, ISSN 0353-4510.

its frontiers and folds through insights from another discipline, interdisciplinarity ensues as a collateral event. Quite often, it is stability of the Archimedean point that has to be given up to experience the shifting of the terrain under one's feet.

To take this further, the best instance of interdisciplinary approach from my experience comes from being very grounded in one's own discipline, understanding its historicity and specificity and then raising certain questions. Suddenly, you would realize that the space offered by your own discipline is not able to contain the answers. And then, from there you move on. So, starting with a set of issues which is specific to your own concerns, without really making a kind of an intentional project out of it, you tend to move towards other disciplines because your own questions would impel you to a crossover. For example, when I was working on the question of art and aesthetics in comparative terms, I was disturbed by the inherent orientalism of the comparative method. Due to the fact that this orientalist method was visible to me in Richard Schechner's interpretation of *'rasa'*, it compelled me to take cognizance of Performance Studies, a field that Schechner came from. Of course, there are practical problems of interdisciplinarity, which we deal with everyday in our day-to-day teaching; our Master's programme at the School of Arts and Aesthetics, JNU, is integrated, and involves all the three disciplines: Visual Studies, Performance Studies and Cinema Studies. It is impossible for one teacher to handle all the three and invariably, many faculty from all the three fields contribute different lectures while the onus of finding connections and differences among these three fields falls on the coordinator of the course.

Sasanka Perera: I think this answers an important issue that we have been grappling with in our approaches to interdisciplinarity. In our journal[24] we seek to create an interdisciplinary forum in the sense that we envisage possibilities of intersecting across human sciences as long as it makes sense to sociology. And we make sure that it does not mean flitting about various disciplines without adequate disciplinary grounding. However, this is not so easy as it sounds, and hence we witness that despite various discussions, sociologists practise and evaluate students squarely within the confines of sociology as conventionally understood. To move ahead, Kanika has a question.

Kanika Rai Dhanda: My question seems to be partly answered by what you said about interdisciplinarity. But does a conversation with one's own discipline actually happen? What kind of knowledge could emerge from the knowledge processes within this kind of dialogue?

Michael Oakeshott in his conceptualization of tradition lays emphasis on a form of conversation wherein individuals and disciplines are in an interaction with each other and culminate in patterns of activities, which are coherent traditions, themselves and not its mere representations. While dialogic aspects may be missing in such a conversation, can it be posed that this however is the nature of knowledge exchange among traditions of academic disciplines? Being an art historian, do you think that questions at this forum from the lens of different academic traditions point towards this concern?

Parul Dave-Mukherji: From time to time, individuals have to have dialogue with their own disciplines and ask where one is going. So I take this question as different from

24. The journal of the Department of Sociology, South Asian University co-published with Sage, is titled *Society and Culture in South Asia*. See http://scs.sagepub.com/ or http://www.sau.int/journal-soc.html .

the last question. It is not a question of interdisciplinarity or of one discipline speaking to another but when one speaks to one's own discipline. I think such conversations are very important. I will address your question with reference to what is happening to feminist art history at the moment. This question came up importantly within Feminist Art History as it was getting formulated in the West during the 1970s. Recently, I came across an essay by an eminent feminist art historian, Griselda Pollock in the *Art Bulletin* journal, which is brought out by the College Art Association, a leading journal for Art History in the USA. To mark its hundred years of being published, it has recently started a new series entitled, '*Whither Art History?*'. Its aim is to raise disciplinary questions like, "Where is art history going?" in an increasingly globalizing world. Pollock threw open a set of questions that compel us to grasp the contemporary reality of feminism. It entailed a staging of a dialogue within Feminist Art History, a discipline that she herself had helped to form since the 1970s. She proceeds by noting how the very questions that feminists started with at the inception of this discipline have changed. They are no longer phrased as: "why there are no women artists?" or "what is the canon and how is it formed?" Now the questions are, "what keeps the canon in place?" and "what accounts for its persistence in the face of massive evidence of international creative art and of histories by both men and women?"

The new set of questions is reflective of the new awareness of altered geopolitics of the globalizing world that have now brought in many more new players who are still not recognized by those in power. The question creates an affiliation of the 'first' world feminism with the one in the 'third' world, and the interplay between gender and race. It questions the hegemony of the Euro-American art world in the face of the arrival of new artists from the non-Western world and the 'discovery' of a new geography of art; till around the last decade of the 20th century, the whole axis of the art world was assumed to lie somewhere in Europe or in the US. But today, contemporary Asian art is a presence to reckon with, not only in terms of art practice but in terms of the art market as well. Shanghai, Tokyo, Delhi, Manila, Seoul, among others, are gaining recognition as venues of Biennales and art fairs. Global art history as an emerging discipline draws out new regions and constituencies of art and different public. In fact, a term—'the global contemporary' coined by German scholars, Hans Belting, Andrea Buddenseig and Peter Weibel and their jointly curated exhibition entitled *When is Now* at the ZKM, Karlsruhe in 2009 attests to the changing equations in the art world.

So coming back to Kanika's question, when a discipline interrogates its own history and framework from within, it points out, as in the case of Pollock's question, the gap between the inherited conceptual frameworks and the ground reality. Without this recognition, there is little scope for new theoretical frameworks to emerge.

Sasanka Perera: There is a whole set of questions on gender which we are going to pose soon. Before that, to make note of something that we may perhaps discuss later, Parul Dave-Mukherji's reference to the decade of the 1980s is crucial. This occasioned a beginning in the changing nature of events, protocols and growing influence of women artists and also the emergence of more nuanced and politically engaged art in South Asia as well.

Parul Dave-Mukherji: (In affirmation) One has to accept the fact that tremendous development has happened ever since. However, the Indian context needs to be specified. Recently, a number of seminars have been held on the long 1980s and this decade has to be related with the Emergency of the earlier decade. The complexity of the public sphere in

India hit many artists, art critics, and I am sure, many social scientists in the face, so to speak. The advent of television made many aware of the role of the media, just as the arrival of caste and gender in the public sphere following the impact of the 'Mandal Commission'[25] held important implications for social sciences in India. Artists like Vivan Sundaram and Bhupen Khakhar alluded to the Emergency and factory strikes in their work. Again, it was in the mid-1980s that the category of women artists came on its own and today its connection with women's movement can be better grasped. In the Indian context, women artists like Nilima Sheikh, Nalini Malani, Arpita Singh, Arpana Caur, Madhavi Parekh, among others experimented with media, often preferring a smaller, intimate scale and even water colours to strike out on their own.

But, to what extent, have women artists impacted the politics of canonization? That remains to be seen. In the West, there had been a major feminist exhibition entitled 'Elles' or 'She' (in the plural) at the Pompidou Centre in 2012 which involved the rehanging of women artists' works from the collection of this contemporary art museum: a plan which at once made visible major gaps in the collection of women's art and thus betrayed the politics of canonization itself.

Sasanka Perera: I was wondering, what kind of people know about this canonization and re-canonization of the 'same old suspects' which often happens due to specific

---

25. This was a commission headed by B.P. Mandal, which advocated reservation of seats for the backward caste groups in education and employment in India. For more information on this, see the commission reports available on the Government of India portal: http://www.ncbc.nic.in/User_Panel/UserView.aspx?TypeID= 1161 (last accessed on 30 August 2015).

choices made by mostly European and North American curators and writers. Is there anything we can do in this situation as consumers?

Parul Dave-Mukherji: I am not sure about what we can do as consumers in a country where culture is a neglected category and features quite low in state priority and the coverage that art gets in newspapers has shrunk to an insignificant position. This sounds too pessimistic. Perhaps the onus is on art historians, writers, critics and curators to contest canonization.

Sasanka Perera: Are we doing it (the requisite) in our part of the world?

Parul Dave-Mukherji: I think it is also a matter of challenging the hegemony and their authority.

Sasanka Perera: That is what I am saying.

Parul Dave-Mukherji: I think it is being done better by artists than art curators and art historians. The risks that many contemporary artists are taking today to shake up established modes of seeing and being in the world is far greater than those who write on art. This is really a moment of auto-criticism. Many artists are less burdened by identity politics and think beyond the national frame. Exceptional curators like Ranjit Hoskote have taken risks by questioning received notions as he did while curating the 2011, Venice Biennale which had an Indian pavilion for the first time. He placed his critique of the nation state within the heart of his curatorial intervention, supported by the state!

To give an example of global cultural politics, let me tell you a little story about how I came to participate in a panel on global art history in 2007. It was a part of a CIHA (International Committee of History of Art) conference in Melbourne, Australia. Prior to that, in 2004, I had chanced upon a book with a fascinating title—*Stories of Art* by James

Elkins in a bookstore in Oxford. It reminded me of E.H. Gombrich's *The Story of Art*, a book that I was enamoured with as an undergraduate, oblivious of its politics of exclusion of non-Western art histories. Noting the shift from the singular, hegemonic *The Story of Art* to *Stories of Art*, I began to expect a radically new take on art history that would be relevant to the multicultural, post-modern world.

However, the book left me deeply disappointed by its insidious ethno-centricism which expressed an acute scepticism about the very category of Non-Western art history. To validate this conclusion, the author in fact referred to the Sanskrit text, the *Citrasutra* of the *Visnudharmottata Purana* which was part of my doctoral work, ironically completed in Oxford. At the CIHA conference, I concentrated on cultural misreading that informed the interpretation of Indian art history and the arrogance of the author to interpolate about Indian art history based on the fragmentary reading of a premodern text in Sanskrit—a language that the author might have/had no expertise in. I partly situated this trend with the 'new knowledge system' facilitated by the internet. With an easy Google access to information, the latter can be paraded as knowledge, and on that basis, you can actually start making pronouncements about a region you don't know at all. Elkins was not present at the CIHA conference, but within a week or so the news must have reached him that this person from India had critiqued his position. I started getting emails from this scholar who assumed that better communication between us would clear my misunderstanding! In all fairness to Elkins, it must be added that each time he revisited the issue of representation of non-Western art history; he acknowledged our exchange and my contribution.

What this demonstrated was the power of critique in Western academia, and how it can function as a way of making our voices heard in that part of the world. However, in the final analysis, such a space of critique is not a productive space as it rarely opens space for dialogue, being compromised by political correctness. Equally important is to turn the same critical gaze at knowledge production in "our" spaces which pose far graver problems in controlling interpretations from a problematic ideological position of rewriting history to suit present identity politics.

Sasanka Perera: One good thing I have noticed is that, because this conversation is so comprehensive thus far, many questions are getting answered in the process even before we formally come to them. And hence it is relevant to shift to other questions which still need to be addressed, which requires shifting of gears. There is this particular question that I am going to read out. This is related to something that Nikos Papastergiadis has said. One of the things he said in his recent book, *Spatial Aesthetics,* is that when art is presented away from galleries in everyday locations and is crafted by using everyday material that may not be typically thought of as art material, it "has created the need for new critical tools to determine its aesthetic value and social meaning." Does it make sense to assume when determining the social meaning of such artworks as well as when locating them more broadly within the contexts of their production that sociology and other disciplines in the social sciences might become useful as a specific discursive practice dealing with human interactions and the work of culture?

And in the same context, I realized that you mentioned at the outset of the conversation about your own institution (School of Arts and Aesthetics, JNU) where the subject of study is not art history, instead it is visual studies, and you perhaps rightly deemed it a novel development. But I was also wondering if it is useful that some of these institutions, such as the one you belong to, might like to or think of teaching subjects like sociology or social anthropology as a way of getting more squarely into visual studies?

Parul Dave-Mukherji: In fact, for me, sociology is a natural ally of art history because of the shared disciplinary interests in the domain of cultural production. Sociology emerged as a major discipline within art history during the 1950s with the publication of Arnold Hauser's multiple volumes on the social history of art that began from the prehistoric period and extended up to the modern age. Prior to this moment, formalism was considered as the most dominant method through which art of any period, time and culture could be explained in terms of shape, line, colour and other such formal constituents.

It was with the British Marxist art historian, T.J. Clark that a significant step was taken in the direction of social art history by the late 1970s. Here, the context of the disenchantment following the failure of the students' rebellion of 1968 in Paris was most relevant. Clark looked back over a century to discover his ideal artist in Gustave Courbet and placed his work in the context of the 1868 revolution. In the decade of the 1970s, the battle lines were drawn between emerging feminism and Marxism and more specifically Griselda Pollock's use of gender in art history and T.J. Clark's sociological method that gave salience to class. Pollock critiqued Clark over the priority that he gave to class over gender and how he did not consider the two analytical categories as mutually inflecting. And in fact at some point, Clark, having read feminist art historians' work, revised his position and admitted his blindness concerning gender. In other words, a sociology of art that overlooks gender cannot adequately perform its role of understanding social relationships as they bear upon notions of the artist as a genius and the politics of representation and reception.

Talking about the Indian context, of course, nationalism and Marxism have been main prisms through which the sociology of art has been theorized in the study of modern Indian art. In this respect, Bengal has been the main reference point whether it is Ratnabali Chatterjee's *From the Karkhana to the Studio: A Study in the Changing Social Roles of Patron and Artist in Bengal* (1990); Tapati Guha Thakurta's *The Making of a New 'Indian' Art: Artists, Aesthetics and Nationalism in Bengal* (1992) or Partha Mitter's *Art and Nationalism in Colonial India* (1994). In the study of modern and contemporary Indian art, Geeta Kapur[26] and Nanda Kumar have touched upon sociology in the manner in which they set up relationships between artistic representation and new notions of citizenship, secularism and patronage that emerged out of colonial modernity. Here, it is important to mention art writing by cultural theorists grounded in critical theory who worked with poststructuralist theories of representation.

Susie Tharu's catalogue essay on N. Pushpamala[27] entitled, '*This is Not an Inventory: Norms and Performance in Everyday Femininity*' (Bangalore: India Foundation for the Arts, 2004) for an exhibition called *Native Women in South India: Manners and Customs* is noteworthy. Adopting the genre of photo-performance, Pushpamala dresses up as different people, sometimes like a famous protagonist from a painting like Ravi Varma's *Lakshmi* or *Saraswati*. She would dress up like goddess Lakshmi and get herself photographed with everything requisite in place. It is regarding such works that Tharu has written extensively and placed it within a

26. See Geeta Kapur's *When was Modernism: Essays on Contemporary Cultural Practice in India* (New Delhi: Tulika, 2000).
27. For a glance at N. Pushpamala's work, see https://www.artsy.net/artist/pushpamala-n (last accessed on 11 September 2015).

'citational practice,' which is defined in the case of Pushpamala's work in terms of how a contemporary artist deliberately revisits the past, almost like a cultural anthropologist, and quotes from it performatively to reflect on the present. Here, I see a connection between anthropology and sociology both in Pushpamala's art practice and Tharu's critical commentary.

This is the sense in which one can reiterate that sociology has always been an ally of art history. The entry of cultural studies into art history, evident in the turn to New Art History around 2000, further underlined the relevance of sociology.

Your reference to the everyday is very relevant. Many contemporary artists today turn to inexpensive, everyday material, much like the artists of the 1960s, from the influential avant garde movement of Arte Povera. Arte Povera has always had a deep resonance in India. Young artists complain of lack of state patronage, infrastructure, etc. and the problem of expensive art material. It is in this context that performance art becomes crucial, as a contemporary artist like Anita Dube declares about this art form as a medium in which, "all you need is your body." Even art galleries have adapted their environment and infrastructure to accommodate contemporary artists' engagement with the everyday. An artist like Riyaz Komu uses simple material. This has also nudged artists into conceptual art. It has not taken off very successfully because patronage from private art galleries has been guarded. There is nothing to sell as conceptual art deliberately demolishes the object through its anti-market stance.

Sasanka Perera: How come then the basics of sociology or anthropology are not taught in major art institutions?

Parul Dave-Mukherji: I will tell you why, as an art historian. Sociology is always admitted into art history more as a methodology than as a discipline. Of all modern sociologists, Pierre Bourdieu's work, particularly *Distinction: A Social Critique of the Judgment of Taste* (1984) has been most influential in art history as it not only offers a resounding critique of Kantian aesthetics, but also allows us to reckon with taste in the domain of popular art.

Sasanka Perera: Kanika you had a question.

Kanika Danda: The imperial assemblage for the Queen's proclamation in colonial India of 1877 had mythical symbols for all princely states. The symbol for Kashmir was arbitrarily drawn as three zigzag lines to create symbolization for the new colonial geography of the Kashmir valley in British India. In this context, how does one conceptualize aesthetics? How is the relation of the artist to the creation of the symbol and the politics of crafting a symbol related to this aesthetic conceptualization? In such a rendering of three lines, is there a possibility of imagining something that is inclined towards politics rather than the intent of aesthetics, and therefore in the domain of a non-aesthetic?

Parul Dave-Mukherji: Kanika, I would like to start with my disagreement with your assumption that aesthetics and politics are a binary. In fact, when I first came to JNU as a professor, I realized that the School of Art and Aesthetics, being a newcomer in an institution like JNU, steeped in Marxism, had to deal with some degree of hostility from other schools. For many in JNU, 'aesthetics' as part of the nomenclature of the school, was hugely problematic because they associated aesthetics with elitism. I remember finding Jacques Rancière's book, *Politics of Aesthetics* very handy as a way of counteracting this facile view of aesthetics. Politics and aesthetics cannot be seen as antithetical to each other, but deeply implicated in one another.

What is the meaning of aesthetics? If you go back to its

Greek etymology—*aesthesis*, it has to do with sense perception. How do we experience through our senses? Defined like this, aesthetics at once allows the political to enter its domain. Just as what Foucault says in his theorization of discourse as embedded in the interplay between knowledge and power, Ranciere seems to apply it to the realm of the sensible. Everyone with a pair of healthy eyes can potentially see the world but not everything in the world is equally visible to all. What you can see and what you cannot see are also historically and politically determined. I am also very happy that as a sociologist, you pay attention to visual semiotics of the Kashmiri symbol. We, art historians, often complain about sociologists that in their hurry to regard art as sociological information, they tend to overlook aesthetics or rather look at it through the materiality of art.

Likewise, as an example, I can also think of the rupee symbol, which I think everybody must have seen; it was recently invented. Now, if you bear that symbol in your mind, I would ask you—is it a purely aesthetic symbol or a political one? It's a very clever graphic design because it's somewhere between *devnagari* (the script of Hindi) '*ra*' and English 'R'. It is political because some feature from *devnagari* has been incorporated. The covert message seems to be that the national currency of India belongs to the majority. Perhaps, that was also one of the reasons why it was accepted. It was considered a successful design. It went down well with the majoritarian cultural visual politics.

In a nutshell, I do not agree with the assumption underlying the question that aesthetics and politics are antinomies.

Sasanka Perera: So, it is not just aesthetics or politics, it is both?

Parul Dave-Mukherji: Yes, it is both simultaneously. This symbol of a rupee note was invented by designers from the Indian Institute of Technology, when the rupee became an international currency.

Sasanka Perera: What about the last part of Kanika's question? Was there anything called non-aesthetic or how does it work?

Parul Dave-Mukherji: Well, it is a good question and can only be answered by turning to the debates around popular visual culture, still a contested site about it being a valid area of study and if it partakes of aesthetics. The anxiety really stems from the hierarchy between 'high' art and popular art. If the former consists of painting, sculpture, murals, etc, the latter would include cinema posters, mass illustrations, movie hoardings, etc. While the former has an established constituency of spectators, art dealers, art historians and critics who write about them and of course the collectors—in short the art world, the popular art is beginning to acquire legitimacy mainly through the high artists' appropriation of popular art. Hence the difference between what is aesthetic and non-aesthetic is linked with the politics of canonization.

Sasanka Perera: When you referred to Pushpamala and suggested that she might also be the postmodern artist, I was wondering whether South Asian Art has entered this phase? Can we talk about South Asia in terms of postmodern art? Or is it that some people merely indulge in some works that might be called postmodern for whatever reason even if the contexts of production and consumption still remain rooted to modernist and even pre-modern conditions?

Parul Dave-Mukherji: For me the idea of postmodern in this part of the world cannot be separated from the idea of postcolonial. In South Asia, postmodern has to be inflected via the postcolonial. The postcolonial and the postmodern rub with each other. Our periodization has to be derived from our geopolitics, the specificities of our history and our colonial past which acts as a common frame of reference. All these terms, to be useful, need to be qualified in terms of our reality. What does 'postmodern' mean for us? In my theorization, I use 'postcolonial' in two senses—hyphenated and non-hyphenated. The hyphenated one, could read like "post (hyphen) colonial". I find both the usages quite useful because when it is non-hyphenated, it is possible for us to read the historical epoch before 1947 in India. The first, the hyphenated one, implies a break between colonial and postcolonial and it was coeval with the 1947 moment. The second, non-hyphenated one, entails the pre-independence (1947) moments. In this sense, the postcolonial did not coincide with the gain of political sovereignty. For example, the rejection of oil painting as a medium encapsulates a postcolonial moment in pre-independent India; it could be deemed a part of the decolonizing drive which happened under cultural nationalism in art schools like Santiniketan. At the same time, one cannot overlook the fact that after 1947, artists looked upon themselves as postcolonial artists. The very first modern art movement after 1947 which was the Progressive Artists' Group in Bombay was premised on the rejection of the Bengal School. They in fact embraced an internationalism, whereby they claimed a parity with Western modernism.

However, it is also important to claim that the Indian modern (and I am sure this may be true of modernism in South Asia), follows a different teleology than that of the Euro-American world. In that sense, the Indian modern had more affinity with the postmodern, given its emergence under colonial modernity. Matters of formal purity and abstraction hardly held the same relevance as in the West.

Figurative was hardly a source of anxiety—in fact, it was almost a cultural compulsion that has had an abiding presence. I realize that before we use the term postmodern, we must qualify it. One of the strands of postmodern I want to stress, following Andreas Huyssen's definition[28] is the end of Western domination, through which it can be related with the term 'postcolonial'. This at once leads us to connect these two terms with another slippery term—'contemporary'. When the 'West' becomes one of the many frames of references for artists in India or South Asia, and not the only one, we enter the contemporary. This is when the West's hegemony is relativized. It is in this context that a South Asian affiliation becomes a possibility.

Sasanka Perera: Now it reminds me of my colleague Jagath Weerasinghe, a Sri Lankan artist writing about contemporary issues on Sri Lankan art. Once he said that there was no such thing as 'Post-modern art' in Sri Lanka, but there was something called 'past-modern'.

Parul Dave-Mukherji: Perhaps, this term may be a way of appropriating the postmodern from the non-Western perspective, and it seems to resonate with what I just said. That is, any kind of postmodern that prefigures the Euro-American model of the modern must be seriously contested. I am not being a nationalist. Of course one can read postmodern/pastmodern in multiple ways. In the West, there is a systematic, teleological logic in which modernism is said to arrive because it is premised on an antinomy with their traditional figurative painting or the history painting and its allied mimetic style of representation.

---

28. Andreas Huyssen, "Mapping the Postmodern" in *The Art of Art History: A Critical Anthology*, Ed. Donald Preziosi, Oxford, OUP, 1998, 329-337.

Underpinning their art historiography as evolved by leading critics and art historians like Alfred Barr and Clement Greenberg, all the trends from the middle of the 19th century starting from Edouard Manet to Jackson Pollock in the middle of the 20th century could be arranged in a line to tell a story of a shift from representation to abstraction. But the modernism in South Asia happened under the aegis of colonial modernity. We had a slight problem with the figurative. We did not conform to the above narrative of progress and therefore the scheme of Western teleology at all. So when the Western avant garde artists were trying to dismantle the figurative under different cultural compulsions, artists in South Asia were quite happy practising it. We came up with our own narratives and reinvented the figurative tradition thereby. In this sense, it is possible to claim that the postmodern/pastmodern arrived in South Asia much before it happened to the West.

Dev Pathak: In your attempt to steer clear of conventional binaries, stemming from both the Eurocentric conceptual formulations on performance (such as performance and *rasa* aesthetics of Richard Schechner) and the nativist subversion which places the non-Western example of art experiences as transcendental (such as A.K. Coomaraswamy), you have duly underlined the necessity for conceptual innovation. Thereby, you coin the neologism of 'performative mimesis', pertaining to the category of 'Anukriti' from the *Natyasastra*, which could perform the Derridian act of deconstructing logocentrism of conventional mimetology.

This seems fairly valid in a postcolonial scheme of analysis wherein, as Bhabha argued—the other and the self are intricately enmeshed. But then, this also runs a risk of its own kind. In combating binaries of the past, we tend to take for granted the politics of hybridity, of being, of aesthetic experiences, as well as conceptual formulations. It exhibits a fear or disdain of the local, the regional and the national as it were, in a creative response (if not reaction) to the obsession with the local which did not heed the complexity of colonial encounters. It also amounts to, what Rustom Bharucha elsewhere breezily called an 'airport view' of reality. Operating from this intellectual liminality, we may seek to overcome the constraints of conceptual binaries. But then, the question is—could we ever be exorcised of the binaries in the logic of everyday life, inclusive of art and aesthetics? How long would we languish in the conceptual scheme of "either traditional or modern, or a bit of both" in our approaches to the performances in time and space?

Parul Dave-Mukherji: It is a methodological question. At the end of the day, we must recognize that binaries cannot be avoided. Binaries are after all, analytical, conceptual tools. But they need to be updated, made contemporary, relevant to our times. They can also work better as relational and non-essentialist. They need to be disturbed and subverted before they are replaced. In Coomaraswamy's times, when the colonial "misrepresentation" of Indian art as irrational and monstrous prevailed, and to fight that cultural bias, he felt compelled to mobilize another binary between the West as a materialist Other and the spiritual/religious/Indic self.

His binaries were strategically and successfully deployed to defend Indian art. He silenced all the critics to the extent that even the West accepted it as truth. What I am trying to say is that at the end of the day, Coomaraswamy was playing into their (Western) game. The rules of the game were still their own. I think a much more radical position would be to reverse the binaries. In fact, when teaching Italian Renaissance art, I realize how important it is to foreground its religious context. It is imperative to acknowledge the complexity in the Western art too, and thus attempt to change the rules of the game. By just inverting the hierarchies, one is not really problematizing the essentialist notions that affect both the parties concerned as they are presented as monolithic wholes.

Inversions rather have to demonstrate how relational oppositions are between religious/secular or rational/irrational. These binaries are now outdated. We are no longer under colonial pressure to authenticate ourselves by their terms. So even when Coomaraswamy thought he was subverting the Western frameworks, he was, in fact, deepening them. Binaries have to be constructed as provisional, historicized, and relational. No culture can be seen as privy to one trait which arises under changing conditions.

Kanika Rai Dhanda: Is there an ethnographic turn in the production of art works? Is this distinctive from the process of understanding art through the space and place of imagining art? If art history draws on the archive of exhibitions, curation and in the form of a space designated for aesthetic preservation, do you think that the process of art history has turned towards ethnography? Secondly, how far is this dialogue possible between the process and product of art?

Parul Dave-Mukherji: It is a very interesting question. In fact, while going through this question, I was immediately reminded of a thought-provoking book by Hal Foster called *The Return of the Real.*[29] In this book, he proposes the idea of the artist as ethnographer in order to discuss the development of art and theory since the 1960s. One broad argument that he makes is about the shift that occurs in the manner artists set aside 'class' difference to explore cultural difference as

29. Hal Foster, *The Return of the Real: The Avant-garde at the End of the Century*, Boston: MIT Press, 1996.

more and more artists began to travel widely. Let's take the example of an artist like Francesco Clemente, who was part of the transavant-garde trend that emerged in Europe by the early 1970s. It was in the 1980s that Clemente travelled to Chennai, worked with local art designers, went to Puri, Orissa, and forged a very interesting collaboration with local artists in this region. Subsequently, without undertaking the physical journey, he would continue with the collaboration through the means of the internet, or some middle men. Following instructions from Clemente, local artists created 'customized' images. The images would be sent to Clemente, who, sitting in his studio, would decide what part of these "made to order" images would work for him and use them as part of his own artwork. So, in that sense, it really turns out that (if we follow Hal Foster's logic) artists began assuming the role of an anthropologist, so to speak, in this clear separation of the field constituted by the native artisan and the studio of the artist.

The way in which Hal Foster imagines artists as ethnographers does not quite work in our socio-cultural context. This is because the question of caste as opposed to class has more relevance and very few contemporary artists have engaged with the class/caste distinction. In this respect, N. Pushpamala's[30] foray into colonial anthropology is almost paradigmatic. In one of her photo performances (it is a part of her project on '*Native Women of South India*'); she dresses herself as a Toda tribal; she darkened her skin colour to fit into the so-called Toda stereotype. By exploring the colonial archives, she arrived at her own language while critiquing colonial stereotyping of the tribal and caste-based identities.

30. For a glance at the ethnographic turn in Pushpamala's work, see http://www.saatchigallery.com/artists/artpages/pushpamala_n_whipf.htm (last accessed on 12 September 2015).

There are quite a few examples one can think of, like the Bangalore-based artist, Anup Matthews who has travelled like an ethnographer with a camera to different parts of South India, photographing bishops, who are made to pose before their institutions as a template for creating multiple versions. He almost appears to produce photographic research on the global reach of Christianity and its attendant multiculturalism.

Sasanka Perera: If you take these kinds of practices as an ethnographic turn, does it happen consciously? Do these artists tend to work as ethnographers? Or is it simply interpreted as 'ethnographic' work due to the process or more precisely due to the seemingly ethnographic residues embedded in their practice? The criticism against Hal Foster is also that his understanding of the ethnographer was quite different from an anthropologist's understanding of someone who practises ethnography.

Parul Dave-Mukherji: In fact, I often face this question raised by you because I adhere to the proposition that ethnography is a productive space from which contemporary artists in India operate. I am always asked: Isn't ethnography something which is not very flattering because it reminds us of a colonial ethnographer who objectified the bodies of people and thereby aided in their subjugation? But when I talk about ethnography and anthropology, I am not referring to the traditional ethnographic anthropology; I am referring to the poststructuralist anthropology of Clifford Geertz and Johannes Fabian. Consequently, many new kinds of contemporary anthropological works have come out where anthropologists are no longer driven by the divide between subjugated natives of the global south and the emancipated ethnographer coming from the global north. They are now duly self-critical, looking at their own social formation and seeing commonalities between the 'ritual' practices of their own metropolitan society and that of non-Western society, and problematize an easy self-other divide.

Sasanka Perera: I would now like to shift this discussion to the questions about engendering art and politics of representation, which are also issues you have worked on. Apoorva, you had a question.

Apoorva Kaul: Indian women are expected to behave like goddesses and espouse divine qualities. However, most visual representations of these goddesses show them as light skinned, sharp featured, with a perfectly proportioned body, be it on calendars or prayer books. So, should all Indian women be fair skinned in order to be virtuous and lucky? To be dark skinned is to be like Kali, an assertive, powerful, and malevolent force, not something which is appreciated in a patriarchal society. Can this cycle of gendered and racist portrayals be broken? How willing do you think will today's artists be in painting a dark skinned Sita and how accepting would be their audience?

Parul Dave-Mukherji: It is a very interesting question, and it leads me to the debates around censorship that has many implications for sociology. Until now, censorship debates around painting of goddesses have revolved around nudity and not skin colour because the latter has not fully entered the public sphere. Do we have a vocabulary to talk about it? Our adverts fully endorse the fair skin and our language continues to naturalize it when we say—"she is dark but beautiful". The fair skin goddess stereotype goes back to paintings and oleographs produced by Ravi Varma and his press and they were widely disseminated in social spaces and even informed the cinematic representation.

Partly, the fixation on light skin colour is a form of our colonial hangover, fuelled by our caste system. In the ancient period, fair skin was hardly a norm. Just see Buddhist fresco paintings in Ajanta which show a variety of skin colours.

Although dark skinned women as beautiful women appear to be celebrated, the principal religious characters are fair skinned like the Boddhisattvas. Of course, the hegemony of the Brahmin ideology must have insidiously played a role over centuries in naturalizing the association of fair skin with beauty and goodness. If you go back to Ravi Varma paintings, this skin colour bias is so clearly inscribed in them. All the goddesses and good women are shown light skinned in Varma's works. (And talking about Sita) his very famous painting called 'Sita in Ashoka Vatika' shows Sita pining for Ram while surrounded by dark skinned and nude demons. It is striking that while nudity of the Indian goddesses drawn or painted by M.F. Husain elicited such wrath from a section of the public, these naked ogresses have never attracted censorship for their dark skinned bodies are taken as 'other' bodies.

Sasanka Perera: So where does this binary come from?

Parul Dave-Mukherji: I cannot blame the British for everything (laughter)! But the fact remains that the colonial rule compelled a defensive response. While Coomaraswamy, as we noted earlier, strategically constructed binaries between the West and Asia, his tilt towards the Brahmin identity can be read as his myopia concerning caste-based hierarchies. If you read Coomaraswamy's conception of a pure Hindu artist or an artisan or what he terms as a *shilpi*, he envisages this figure along Brahmanic identity which conformed to his association of purity with art. A *shilpi*, according to him, before starting to paint, had to have a bath, wear white clothes and put on the sacred thread. Before starting to paint or sculpt, he had to bend down before the elders to seek their blessings.

While some of it is drawn from the *Shilpa Shastras* or the treatises on art, not everything is explained by them. It is interesting for us to note how the gaps within the text are filled in by Coomaraswamy's imagination of a perfect traditional society. Of course, Coomaraswamy can hardly be the only factor in erecting these binaries as typical of the Indic society whose art and culture he was exploring. 'Indic society' was itself steeped in centuries of social, economic and political hierarchies.

Sasanka Perera: Ratan, you had a question on the female body.

Ratan Kumar Roy: In most visual productions (soap operas, advertisements, movies, music videos, etc.), the female body is represented as a mode of fulfilling audiences' (male) pleasure. How do feminist scholars or social scientists respond do this popular way of commodifying the female body?

Parul Dave-Mukherji: My response would again be the same as my answer to the question about skin colour. I remember, as I was teaching a course on Modern Western Art in Baroda, we were talking about a famous painting by Edouard Manet called Olympia.[31] It is a painting that has a white nude woman reclining on a bed in the foreground while her black maid brings to her a bouquet of flowers sent by her client. Here, 'Olympia', rather than being a sacred Greek goddess refers to a 19th century prostitute in a Parisian brothel. The painting was shown in a French salon in the middle of the 19th century where it gave rise to heated controversies, having touched upon the moral ambivalence of the French bourgeois society.

In the classroom, I would often ask a student volunteer to come up to the board[32] and sketch a diametrically opposite

---

31. Olympia is a famous painting by Édouard Manet; see http://www.jssgallery.org/other_artists/manet/olympia.htm (last accessed on 12 September 2015).
32. This belongs to a time when I would use a black board, and not a power point presentation for teaching – Parul Dave-Mukherji

image of Manet's Olympia in terms of its gender and race relationship. Of course, it was a very difficult exercise for all of us—to think and draw the opposite of Manet's white nude. Often, students got it right when they would draw a black male body reclining in that posture, taking the place of Olympia, after overcoming a great deal of conceptual difficulty! This conditioning, as pointed out by the feminist art historian, Griselda Pollock, extends to our common parlance. The term 'old master' loses its connotation of a great genius when it undergoes a gender translation into 'old mistress'.

The feminist project has to begin with the very language that we use inevitably to talk about art and be aware of asymmetries that are inscribed in language itself. More pertinent to your question, the other realm that invites a feminist occupation is desire itself that has traditionally been appropriated as a male domain. In Indian literature, critical studies carried out by Susie Tharu and others have addressed the question of female desire in the poetry of Akka Mahadevi and other women writers in the past. In contemporary art, Tejal Shah has complicated feminist questions by extending the domain of inquiry into transsexual and same sex identities using photographs, videos and performances.

Manoj Dhakal: In the context of globalization, local art and culture do not always remain static; rather, they interact with other cultures. Can there then, be the possibility of seeing 'unique national/local art' when two or more contexts have proximity, not just politically but also in religious and cultural terms?

Parul Dave-Mukherji: Yes. The phenomenon of globalization has compelled us to regard culture or cultures in a dynamic sense. I am reminded of Arjun Appadurai's work on the cultural impact of globalization which he envisages through multiple scapes and thus drawing from spatial metaphors. However, we must also acknowledge that the mobility of culture has always existed, even in pre-modern times, captured by the term-transcultural. Any mapping of, say, Buddhism, outside India through shifting iconography has to take cognizance of the transcultural. It is amazing as to how the figure of Bodhisattva not only assumes different cultural aspects of dress, ornaments but also its gender identity as it traverses across many cultures; by the time, it travels to China and Japan, the Bodhisattva transmutes into a female character, Guanyin. What separates our times of globalization from the former mobility of culture through trade, religion and war is the speed with which images and ideas travel aided by the technology of the internet and virtual connectivity travel/move across the globe. What used to take centuries or decades, now happens within a week. So I think trans-culturalism becomes a very important theoretical trope that allows us to fathom this mobility. However, it has to be seen both in terms of art works travelling either as physical objects when they take part in international exhibitions or as virtual images or the speed with which artists are now travelling.

The question of a distinct, unique national art can also be seen as a statement of power and ideology, and we have to ask whose interest is being served by making such claims.

Sasanka Perera: Isn't travel an abiding feature of artists and art-production in South Asia since recent times? It seems to me that the ability to travel across the region since the 1980s or so has allowed for the emergence of a clear discourse on art in South Asia if not a specific kind of art. I wonder how local ideas might manage their identity in the wake of the global and the regional which seem to be omnipresent.

Parul Dave-Mukherji: There are interesting ways in which, under this new situation, whatever you call it, the local has earned actually new visibility; this was followed up or subsumed by the national earlier. At present, local can find a new sense of liberation at odds with 'national'. I remember the group of artists which was called the 'Kerala Radicals'; they were Marxists in orientation; the group came to Baroda once; they are very anti-art establishment, especially against the canon makers. When they got a chance to travel across Europe for the first time, without any funding agencies supporting them, they could manage to establish direct contacts with art institutions in various countries they were going to visit. It was only possible in the age of the internet. In this sense, the internet has been very liberating for various artists. Many artists in India did not get any visibility because their works did not win the approval of the canon makers or the gate keepers of modern and contemporary art. When foreign curators visited India, they were officially instructed to connect with the usual suspects and a select group of artists who one predictably expects to see at the Biennales. Such a situation creates conditions for the recanonization of the canonized! But the new media wave and the internet have altered the rules of the game and made possible new dynamics of canonization. Under these conditions, it is possible for a local artist to connect with the global art-world and bypass the national.

Sasanka Perera: Pooja, you may ask your question.

Pooja Kalita: We have always known that an artist makes or portrays what he or she feels like expressing. In that sense, does she or he have to go through any dilemma in terms of responsibilities of representation? For example, in the case of gender, a girl can either be a subject towards sexuality or objectification of the body.

Parul Dave-Mukherji: It is an interesting question on a problematic issue. I take it as an issue of agency of representation by a woman artist. If the theme concerns the body, how does a woman artist go about it? How does she handle the portrayal of male or female nudes? There is a very interesting book called *The Colonial Harem* by the Algerian culture theorist, Malek Allouala that appeared in 1987.[33] The book takes up 19th century postcards produced by French photographers featuring Algerian women. Steeped in French orientalism, these postcards were in circulation at the time when Algeria was a French colony. They capture the colonial desire to enter the forbidden space of a harem and the French photographers made the local prostitutes pose as *harem* women in a mis-en-scene in their studios. What appeared as a feminist critique of the postcards by Alloula was challenged by Rey Chow. Chow pointed out the contradiction in the book in the way the postcard images were used as a way of exposing the French gaze. Alloula's claim to return the gaze was channelled by exposing the bodies of Algerian women, ending up objectifying them again. In a sense, it raises an important ethical issue and makes us aware of the thin line dividing the space of objectification and that of the critique.

This is one of the reasons why many feminist conceptual artists, such as Anita Dube[34] in India, have been cautious about their use of the woman's body in their art. They refrain from showing the female body as a whole and instead, prefer fragments; of course, fragments as such are no less problematic as they can heighten the fetishization of the body. Dube reaches out for a deeper level than that of the body. In her *Blood Wedding* series made in 1997, she wrapped human bones in red velvet and created aesthetic objects out of them, ornamenting the surface with beads. At another level, they work like memento moris or reminders of the fragility and

33. Malek Alloula. 1987. *The Colonial Harem.* Manchester: Manchester University Press.
34. For a glimpse of Anita Dube's works, see http://www.saffronart.com/artists/anita-dube (last accessed on 21 September 2015).

transcience of the human body—a fact that the ideology of capitalism works against in its bid to celebrate the simultaneity of the present. So an artist like Dube not only touches upon feminism in its handling of body fragments but offers a critique of capitalism in the way she addressed temporality.

Sasanka Perera: But in the case of Anita Dube's specific work you refer to, and I have seen pictures of it, I was wondering why she was doing that; what her politics were? I could see issues such as the commentaries on the fragility of the human body and so on. But what about the ethics of handling human remains, that are not your own, you know what I mean? Every culture has a corpus of ethical practices to deal with these issues. I am not sure if an artist like Dube has adequately dealt with this, irrespective of whatever other nuances that might emerge from her work.

Parul Dave-Mukherji: In fact, this work has remained within India. Since it consists of human bones, she is never likely to get customs clearance!

Sasanka Perera: Because they have parts of a human body or bodies!

Parul Dave Mukherji: Yes. Anita Dube was the daughter of a medical doctor and as a child, she was always fascinated by the skeleton and this experience stayed with her as a way of dealing with melancholy.

Sasanka Perera: A slight shift in our journey with the next question from Kanika.

Kanika Rai Dhanda: How does the discipline of art history perceive the representation of artists' context in digital art? How does the space of the internet and the visual medium impact negotiation with places of consumption at the level of self, its immediacy and temporality?

Parul Dave-Mukherji: Well, digital art has really opened up a totally new way of practice, redefining issues of temporality and the materiality of the medium. Artists have to grapple with virtual space and regard the mediation of technology as an enabling factor. Digital art is squarely located within what Derrida would call, the realm of the iterable, it has given a big blow to the artists' notion of themselves as a genius. Digital art is contingent upon a computer and predesigned programs. In other words, artists have to let their creativity-led information pass through a pattern set by software. No wonder, many digital art theorists have been turning back to the British analytical philosopher, Nelson Goodman's distinction between the autographic and the allographic and how they map on to the analogue and the digital.

Digital art draws attention to the difference between the visual and the verbal. A script consists of letters that necessarily have gaps between them and follow a code. However versatile the medium of digital art may be, with its dependence on artificial memory and technological functions, a digital artist also has to deal with the loss of the organic way of creating. There cannot be accidental dropping of inks because the entire work is mediated. However, where does this digital come from? It comes from fingers, digits; you have to use fingers, apply pressure on information conveyed through the apparatus. The advantage of working with digital is that it has enormous, almost infinite range of numbers of people that you can include in your orbit. The other advantage is speed, the speed at which this information or artworks could move.

Where digital art is at a disadvantage is in the context of the constant threat of obsolescence that it faces. If one part in the whole apparatus is outdated, the whole thing is declared as redundant. This poses a big challenge, and this is the reason why it is not art-market-friendly. Collectors are very reluctant to invest in digital art. Notwithstanding the disadvantages, digital art is much more democratic. Mostly, the artists working with the digital tend to work as a collective. They maintain a deliberate policy that they are not going to leave the signature on any of their artworks. Whatever they do, they do it as a collective. This is unlike the artists in the past where there was a great sense of pride about the individual artistic labour, and their work was considered authentic only when they left their signature on the works.

Today, many artists are very aware of their ethics and responsibilities and the role they have to play in their communities. Amar Kanwar[35], the documentary filmmaker, and Sheba Chhachhi, an installation artist, use digital art as a medium to increase their reach to the wider public (not just the art public), and combine the roles of art practitioners and activists. Raqs Media Collective and CAMP have taken digital art to another level in the way they unite artmaking and art discourse.

Sasanka Perera: When digital art came of age, was there any kind of critical debate asking whether digital was a work of art in the first place? After all, what is considered art has been a perennial anxiety whenever innovations have been introduced into art practice. I am referring particularly to South Asia.

Parul Dave-Mukherji: More than digital art, what spurred critical debate and heated exchanges was installation as an art form in the early 1990s, although today it is difficult to keep installation and digital as separate. *Art India* carried a debate between Anita Dube, who was in favour of installation as a relevant art form, and Anjolie Ela Menon

35. Amar Kanwar's range of work has ben stupendous. See http://amarkanwar.com/ (last accessed on 22 September 2015).

who lambasted it as an import from the West[36]. Menon was, at that time, the highest selling easel painter. Many easel painters were defensive about their medium as it risked getting declared as outdated. The whole debate was couched in nationalist sentiment in the way installation art was seen as something that was imposed from the outside, and therefore un-Indian. Today the whole dynamics has changed as has the art market that has been badly affected by recession. Such times augur well for experimental art, and today very few will question the relevance of installation art, given that it has become a part of the art world in India. Installation, along with digital art, alludes to the aesthetic of immersion and calls for a new mode of viewership.

Apoorva Kaul: In a largely changed social and cultural situation, with new modes of doing art in vogue, how does the conventional art practice survive? What are the changes the conventional art-practice has adopted?

Parul Dave-Mukherji: It is interesting that you raise this question. The Indian art scene is full of contradictions and defies a linear logic of time and trends. While the new media is much talked about and has attained high visibility in India and abroad (the Raqs Media Collective recently had a mid-career retrospective at the NGMA, New Delhi), the trend of easel painting continues, and finds an easy ally in the installation art form. It is possible to arrange paintings on various surfaces and formats in the form of an installation and be counted as contemporary. Manu Parekh is an example of such an artist who had reinvented his style of painting via installation while Gulam Sheikh has embraced a wide range encompassing both painting and digital art.

36. For a brief glimpse of Menon's works, see http://www.saffronart.com/artists/anjolie-menon (last accessed on 22 September 2015).

Ratan Kumar Roy: Experiencing the long cultural history of feudalism, colonialism, post-colonialism, globalization and free market mechanisms, how do we characterize the distinctiveness of visual culture in South Asia? Can we draw any chronology or a structural paradigm to characterize the South Asian visual culture?

Parul Dave-Mukherji: For me it is very important because we are at a very important juncture at the present time. It is at this historical moment that the existence of the South Asian University has become a possibility, revealing that we are a part of a qualitatively different geo-politics. For me, it is very important to radically question eurocentricism, and one of the ways in which we can do this is to engage with the region in this geopolitical sense and create networks of affiliation across South Asia. The idea of a chronological sequence, which you mentioned in your question, really arises from a eurocentric understanding of history. We need not follow that at all because the events unfolding in this part of the world could not be explained by the modes of analyses which were developed elsewhere. On the one hand, it is important to underline commonalities that bind us across South Asia like uneven modernization and the glaring gap between the vernacular and the cosmopolitan in various parts of South Asia. At the same time, the region need not be simplistically reduced to many nations and South Asia does not have to be seen merely as a monolith either. It must be a flexible construct that allows for differences to emerge.

The role of KHOJ in bringing the region of South Asia closer through their various art projects needs to be acknowledged. What does it mean to think about South Asia at this historical juncture is important to reckon with. How does South Asia as a region relate with the global south? Do the biennales in Kochi, Havana and Shanghai speak to each other without Western mediation? Is the separation of the global south and global north a productive division or are we witnessing a new segregation and polarization that need to be resisted? The framework of 'region' that was once an empowering term to critique the hegemony of the national modern is once again becoming fraught with both new possibilities and threats at once.

Sasanka Perera: I think there is another dimension through which to think about it. For instance, whenever we flippantly talk about South Asian art, cinema or identity, do we really mean what South Asia means intellectually as opposed to an often contested amalgamation of geographic units? In the same manner, we can also ask the question as to why the idea of South Asian University is significant; the idea might not exist in any kind of formal or practical system of thinking beyond a point. What is South Asian in the South Asian University beyond its name for instance? And that is the struggle for many who subscribe to the idea. It is a struggle that needs to continue.

Let me now bring this conversation to an end, though I know that the questions we raised and the sort of responses we received would need more conversations and more deliberations to iron out more seriously. But I am happy that we have begun a much needed journey today through this conversation. Finally, I just want to thank all of you for your active and nuanced participation. Hopefully we will continue to discuss these issues as time passes.

Conclusion:
Towards an Inconclusive Closure

A possible closure for a conversation such as the one you have gone through will always entail a 'hereafter', a potential continuity with loose strands, a perpetuity of engagement with the questions, answers and deliberations. Also, there is another significant disclaimer hovering the closure here: there are too many beans spilled in the conversation to be gathered by an editor to present in a neatly summed up conclusion. Hence, editorial humility is the only available heuristic scheme of drawing this provisional closure to the conversation.

As a modest wish-fulfilment, it could be mentioned that the conversation has underlined some frequently occurring issues related to the intersections between sociology, arts and art history. Namely, one of them, very prominent in this conversation is the modes of interdisciplinary dialogue among scholars of sociology, social anthropology, art history, cultural studies, and performance studies. Despite a fairly lucid explanation on the 'good' and 'bad' ways of interdisciplinary dialogues, it must not be shocking to come across more fogginess pertaining to the issue. After all, many such ideas are easier said than done, in the wake of manifold institutional resistances and inability of the policy-making educational administrators to fathom the intricacies of the practices involved. Could interdisciplinary dialogue be an institutionalized practice? And if this was possible, what would be the nature and scope of such an institutionalized practice? Simply, what would be the formally acknowledged nature and scope of the interdisciplinary dialogue? Unfortunately, institutions such as the University Grants Commission in the region of South Asia, or administrators in various varsities in the region, may have fairly simplistic or perhaps allegedly spurious notions of what is meant by interdisciplinary dialogue. The question indeed calls for further deliberations: How can we be interdisciplinary without falling prey to the allegedly misleading utopias inherent in it and with a full awareness of the complexity of the practice?

Yet another dimension of this conversation is a quest of shared subjects and objects of study for the various disciplines such as art history, cultural study, performance studies and sociology. The issue of representation of sexuality, stereotypes, and dynamics of power relations in the works of art are perhaps where interdisciplinary interests might meet. Similarly, the issue of a non-Eurocentric epistemology is a common interest for the disciplines flagged in this conversation. Many waters have flown ever since post-colonial critiques of Eurocentric theorizing surfaced, adding more decibels to the proposition towards provincializing Europe. But then, debates have evoked critical rethinking on the category of indigeneity too. This has led to the dictum, 'neither unreflective borrowing of theories and concepts nor subscription to epistemological nationalism (localism)'! This critical realization perhaps solicits more from a conversation to reflect on the dynamics of local and global, national and trans-national, and also intra-dynamic regional. The simplistic binaries are perhaps too outdated to aid in discusrive departures from Eurocentric theorizing, and hence a simple appeal of 'provincializing Europe' may not be adequate for the contemporary order of knowledge production.

Meanwhile, there is also an exceedingly clear understanding that replacing Eurocentric thinkers with global South Asian thinkers makes little dent in the structural hegemony in the production and circulation of knowledge. A thinker located in the geographical location of South Asia, ruminating and proposing antitheses, may seldom match the outreach of their louder counterparts in the geographical location in the West. Would interdisciplinary dialogues be interested in engaging with the power structures that determines the nature and scope of researching, writing, teaching, etc.?

This conversation has amply emphasized the politics of re-canonization and circulation of artists and art-scholars. And in this wake, it is pertinent to add further questions to the issue of epistemological revisiting. For instance, the epistemological propositions of thinkers from the global south could also delimit the imagination of social, cultural and political realities of their own context. Finally, a further engagement with the idea of shared subject and object of study in various disciplines is warranted. The mere instance of interaction of society and artists in the wake of the ethnographic turn in the world of art does not adequately elucidate the intricate meanings of the interaction. Perhaps, an anthropologist will have due reservations about the use of the term 'ethnographic', and would be keen to bring in the complications pertaining to the ethnographic practice into the discourse. The latter, in this scheme, would not be an apolitical and innocent paradigm; it would instead be deemed as a political act on the part of the ethnographer geared towards engendering meanings. It applies to colonial as well as postcolonial contexts.

With this very incomplete and evidently inadequate summing up, primarily to underline the necessity of the perpetuity of this conversation and its 'hereafter'. It is seemingly safe to rest the case on this note.